# OUTFITSOPEDIA

## *The Basics*

Hannah B.

This book is dedicated to my mother, Teresita, who started me on my fashion journey at a very young age. Love you, mom.

# Prologue

Have you ever looked in your closet and yet cannot find anything to wear? Have you been buying the same gray sweater/white tee/dark jeans over and over again? Do you find yourself buying just whatever you fancy without a plan? Most of us do.

Like most women, I have amassed a lot of clothes that I cannot get rid of. They all spark joy.

In an effort to save time and money (and the planet, too), I told myself I should only buy the things I need and just use whatever I have in my closet, mix and match them, and create outfit ideas.

In this book, I have made a list of the core pieces every woman should have in her wardrobe, some outfit combinations for each season, and a list of the most common pieces that can be mixed and matched with the core pieces to create more outfits. I recommend that you go through each piece and buy only the ones you see yourself wearing about 100 times.

I hope that this book can save you money, save you time deciding what to wear in the morning, and save the planet by reducing waste.

So many clothes, so little time.

Just wear what makes you happy.

Hannah B.

# Table of Contents

# Core Pieces

## CORE PIECES

These are the pieces every woman needs in her wardrobe. With these, you can create outfits appropriate for most dress codes and any season. If you are looking to be a minimalist, these may be all you need.

Always make sure your clothes are in good condition, clean, and well pressed.

1. Black suit jacket or black cardigan - A black suit jacket is always a staple on interviews and always looks smart but if you find yourself wearing cardigans more, get a black cardigan instead.

2. Denim jacket - Make your outfit more casual by wearing a denim jacket over it.

3. Black leather jacket - Effortlessly cool.

4. Trench coat - In beige, please.

5. Black wool coat - A winter staple.

6. Black camisole/tank.

7. White tee (round or V-neck).

8. Striped top.

9. White button-down shirt.

10. Black turtleneck long sleeve.

11. Little black dress - Sheath, shift, or A-line.

12. Black suit skirt - Pencil, straight, or A-line.

13. Black suit pants - In a tapered cut that can go with both heels and flats.

14. Dark wash jeans - In a style that can go with both heels and flats, like high-rise skinny jeans or mom jeans.

15. Black jeans - Again, in a style that can go with both heels and flats.

16. Black swimsuit - In solid black with no patterns.

17. Caftan - To wear over your swimsuit or by itself.

18. Denim shorts - In a style that is not too short, like mom shorts.

19. Thong sandals - In black or beige, waterproof.

20. Black ballet flats.

21. White sneakers - In a style that looks good on you.

22. Nude pumps - With a pointy toe.

23. Black pumps - With a pointy toe.

24. Black ankle boots.

25. Black open-toe heels.

26. Black evening clutch.

27. Black everyday bag.

28. Black medium-sized cross-body bag.

29. Black tote bag.

30. Bag organizer.

31. Black oversized sunglasses.

32. Black collapsible umbrella.

33. Water bottle - Bring a reusable one wherever you go.

34. Silk scarf - Always keep one handy.

35. Simple studs (diamonds, pearls, gold, or silver).

36. Personal jewelry (engagement ring, wedding ring, etc.)

37. Watch - With black leather or metal straps. Two-tone (silver and gold) metal straps are more versatile.

38. Black skinny belt.

39. Black fleece-lined tights or black stockings.

# Outfits

Using the core pieces, the following are some of the outfits you can create, organized by dress code and by season. Wear black fleece-lined tights with dresses and skirts in winter. If an outfit is too plain, accessorize.

## SPRING/ FALL CASUAL 1

# SPRING/ FALL CASUAL 2

# SPRING/ FALL CASUAL 3

# SPRING/ FALL CASUAL 4

## SPRING/ FALL CASUAL 5

# SPRING / FALL CASUAL 6

# SPRING/ FALL CASUAL 7

# SPRING/ FALL CASUAL 8

## SPRING / FALL CASUAL 9

# SPRING/ FALL CASUAL 10

## SPRING/ FALL CASUAL 11

# SPRING/ FALL CASUAL 12

# SPRING/ FALL CASUAL 13

# SPRING/ FALL CASUAL 14

## SPRING/ FALL CASUAL 15

# SPRING/ FALL CASUAL 16

## SPRING/ FALL CASUAL 17

## SPRING/ FALL CASUAL 18

# SPRING / FALL CASUAL 19

## SPRING/ FALL CASUAL 20

# SPRING / FALL CASUAL 21

# SPRING/ FALL CASUAL 22

## SPRING/ FALL CASUAL 23

## SPRING/ FALL SMART CASUAL 1

# SPRING/ FALL SMART CASUAL 2

## SPRING / FALL SMART CASUAL 3

## SPRING / FALL SMART CASUAL 4

# SPRING/ FALL SMART CASUAL 5

# SPRING/ FALL SMART CASUAL 6

## SPRING/ FALL SMART CASUAL 7

# SPRING / FALL SMART CASUAL 8

## SPRING / FALL SMART CASUAL 9

# SPRING/ FALL BUSINESS 1

## SPRING / FALL BUSINESS 2

# SPRING/ FALL BUSINESS 3

## SPRING/ FALL BUSINESS 4

# SPRING/ FALL BUSINESS 5

## SPRING/ FALL BUSINESS 6

## SPRING/ FALL BUSINESS 7

## SPRING/ FALL BUSINESS 8

## SUMMER - BEACH

# SUMMER CASUAL 1

## SUMMER CASUAL 2

# SUMMER CASUAL 3

## SUMMER CASUAL 4

# SUMMER CASUAL 5

## SUMMER CASUAL 6

# SUMMER CASUAL 7

## SUMMER CASUAL 8

# SUMMER CASUAL 9

# SUMMER CASUAL 10

## SUMMER CASUAL 11

## SUMMER CASUAL 12

## SUMMER CASUAL 13

## SUMMER SMART CASUAL 1

## SUMMER SMART CASUAL 2

# SUMMER SMART CASUAL 3

## SUMMER SMART CASUAL 4

# SUMMER SMART CASUAL 5

## SUMMER SMART CASUAL 6

## SUMMER SMART CASUAL 7

## SUMMER BUSINESS 1

## SUMMER BUSINESS 2

## SUMMER BUSINESS 3

## SUMMER BUSINESS 4

## SUMMER BUSINESS 5

## SUMMER BUSINESS 6

# WINTER 1

## WINTER 2

You can use the above as a guide for everyday dressing, swap heels for flats for comfort, skip the ones you do not like, photocopy this book and cross out the ones you have tried, or use the outfit templates for your other clothes as illustrated below.

# Extras

## EXTRAS

The following is a checklist of the most common pieces of clothing that you can add to your wardrobe. See which ones you need for your lifestyle.

## UNDERGARMENTS

☐ Smooth nude bra - To wear under all your clothes, especially if your top is slightly see-through

☐ Nude convertible bra - To wear with your strapless/halter/one shoulder tops

☐ Black convertible bra - To wear with black tops, especially knitted ones

☐ Black lace bra

☐ Boob tape

☐ Nipple covers

☐ Invisible lift-up adhesive nipple cover

☐ Lace-up self-adhesive bra - For the ultimate push-up

☐ Self-adhesive silicone push-up bra

☐ Bra converting clip - To turn your regular bra into a racerback bra

☐ Bra extender hook strap

☐ Clear bra straps - If you need to wear a bra but don't want the straps to show

☐ Seamless panties

☐ Black lace panties

☐ High waist shapewear panties

☐ Shapewear shorts

☐ Short cycling shorts - In nude or black. To wear under short dresses and skirts

☐ Cotton socks - Sneaker liner socks or thick socks, depending on what you need

☐ Black sheer stockings

☐ Black opaque tights

☐ Fishnets

☐ Black stockings and garter belt

☐ Body and clothing tape

## LOUNGE

☐ Sweat suit - In black, gray, etc.

☐ Velvet sweat suit

☐ Tees - In black, white, etc. Plain tees are more versatile

☐ Sweat shorts - In black, gray, etc. For summer

☐ Jersey leggings

☐ Camo sweat pants

☐ Caftan

☐ Pajamas

☐ Cotton robe

- ☐ Slippers

## GYM

- ☐ Gym clothing
- ☐ Trainers
- ☐ Gym bag

## NIGHT OUT

Black is always a good choice.

- ☐ One-shoulder top - Sleeveless or long sleeve
- ☐ Cutout top
- ☐ Mesh top - To wear over tubes, camis, etc.
- ☐ Lace top
- ☐ Lace camisole
- ☐ White tank
- ☐ White mini skirt
- ☐ Black leather mini skirt
- ☐ Mini skirt - Solid-colored, patterned, bodycon, pleated
- ☐ Bodycon dress - Under a coat or jacket

☐ Stilettos - Also nice in red, fuchsia, nude, metallic colors. Can be lacy, strappy, with rhinestones, etc.

☐ Sandals with high heels - If you cannot wear stilettos

☐ Pointy boots - Over-the-knee, knee, ankle boots

☐ Any shoe with an ankle wrap - In nude or a color close to your skin tone. Other colors might work but make sure the straps are thin.

## WINTER

☐ Sweaters - Fair Isle, cable-knit, etc.

☐ Sweater dress - Looks good with tights and a belt

☐ Parka - Preferably with fur

☐ Puffer coat - When it is too cold outside

☐ Slim puffer coat - To wear under your other coats that are not warm enough for the weather

☐ Toque

☐ Neck warmer

☐ Scarf

☐ Mittens or gloves - Use waterproof ones with 3M Thinsulate for harsh winters.

☐ Black fleece-lined leggings - To wear under your jeans when it is too cold

☐ Skin-tone fleece tights - To wear under skirts and dresses when it is too cold. You can wear sheer or opaque black stockings over them, too.

☐ Fleece-lined tights - To wear with your sweater dresses

- ☐ Thermal socks - Cotton socks are not appropriate for winter
- ☐ Snow boots - For harsh winters.

## SUMMER

White is a good choice for summer. In cotton or linen.

- ☐ Summer crop top
- ☐ Off-shoulder top
- ☐ Kimono
- ☐ Denim vest - In light wash, mid wash, dark wash, etc.
- ☐ Little white dress - Sleeveless, with sleeves, smocked, flowy, etc.
- ☐ Maxi dress - In black
- ☐ Chambray or denim shirtdress
- ☐ T-shirt dress - In neutral colors, stripes, etc.
- ☐ Midi dress - In neutral colors, stripes, florals, etc.
- ☐ Rompers - In white, black, chambray, olive, etc. Can be strapless, with spaghetti straps, lacy, floral, etc.
- ☐ Jumpsuit - In black
- ☐ Denim skirt - Not too short
- ☐ White mini skirt - Again, not too short.

☐ Overalls - Can be skirt overalls or short overalls

☐ Skort - In denim or black

☐ Denim shorts - In light wash, mid wash, dark wash, white, black. Not too short

☐ Paper-bag shorts - In white, black, beige, denim, etc.

☐ Shorts - In neutral colors, pinstripes, floral, etc.

☐ Tailored shorts - For more formal summer events. Get them in black, white, cream, etc.

☐ Shorts suit

☐ Bikinis - In solid colors or in patterns. Mix and match

☐ Rash guard

☐ Waterproof shorts

☐ Sarong

☐ Water shoes

☐ Flat sandals - Metallic, gladiator, etc.

☐ Thong sandals - In solid or metallic colors

☐ Wedge espadrilles - In nude, black, metallic

☐ Panama hat or floppy straw hat

☐ Straw bag. A tote or a round cross-body

## OCCASIONAL

- ☐ Sheath, shift, A-line, or wrap dresses - These styles are flattering on almost any body type and appropriate for almost any occasion.
- ☐ Cocktail dress - The plainer, the more versatile. Change your look by changing your accessories.
- ☐ Evening gown - Get something you feel gorgeous in.

## GLAM

- ☐ Fur coat - In black, white, leopard, etc.
- ☐ Brown teddy coat
- ☐ Glittery cardigan - In gold, silver, etc.
- ☐ Fur vest
- ☐ Sequined top - In silver, gold, etc.
- ☐ NYE dress - In gold, silver, etc. Also good for cocktails
- ☐ Evening gown - In metallic colors
- ☐ Heels - In silver, gold, etc.
- ☐ Evening clutch - In gold, silver, or rhinestone

## TRAVEL

- ☐ Rain jacket
- ☐ Fleece jacket - Can also be worn under rain jackets for colder weather

☐ Convertible top

☐ Convertible dress/skirt

☐ Khaki skort

☐ Yoga shorts or pants

☐ Jazz pants

☐ Convertible pants/shorts

☐ Short/long black leggings

☐ Travel money belt - To wear under your (loose) top. Keep your passport, credit cards, and cash safe. Get one with an RFID blocker. Must not be visible when in public. Use a decoy wallet instead.

☐ Black shoulder bag with zipper - Carry them close to your body.

☐ Overnight bag

☐ Backpack

☐ Wheeled carry-on - So you do not have to worry about lost luggage or wait for your luggage

☐ Black pashmina/blanket scarf - To use on long flights and while sightseeing

## VERSATILE PIECES

Pieces you can mix and match with your core pieces for most of the year.

☐ Blazer - In white, gray, beige, etc. Makes any outfit dressier

☐ Black tuxedo jacket

☐ Oversized cardigan - In gray, etc.

☐ Cardigans - In white, solid colors, leopard, etc.

☐ Cabin cardigan

☐ Long cardigan - In gray or black

☐ Zippered hoodie - In black, etc.

☐ Bomber jacket - In black, leopard, etc.

☐ Varsity jacket

☐ Safari jacket

☐ Hooded jean jacket - In Sherpa, fleece, or cotton

☐ Leather jacket - In beige, white, etc.

☐ Aviator jacket - In black, brown, etc.

☐ Olive parka

☐ Trench coat - Black, red, etc.

☐ Coat - In camel, plaid, bold colors, etc.

☐ Camisoles - In white, black, with patterns, lacy, etc.

☐ Tank tops - In black, solid colors, etc.

☐ Tees - In black, gray, blush, etc. Round or V-neck

☐ Raglan tee

☐ Camo tee

☐ Graphic tees - Of your university, favorite band, or fandom

☐ Henley - In white, gray, black, etc. Long or short sleeves

☐ Polo shirt - In white, navy, etc.

☐ Silk tops - In white, black, etc.

☐ Solid-colored tops (turtle, mock turtle, scoop, V, square, sweetheart necklines)

☐ Striped tops

☐ Floral tops

☐ Safari top

☐ Lace or eyelet top - In white or black

☐ Peplum top

☐ White sleeveless button-down shirt

☐ White button-down shirt with short sleeves

☐ White pussy bow blouse

☐ Jewel-toned blouses

☐ Chambray shirt

☐ Button-down shirt - In plaid flannel, black, striped, etc.

☐ Silk button down shirt - In white, black, etc.

☐ Bodysuits - Cami, ruffled, scoop neck, V-neck, square neck, turtleneck in white, black, etc.

☐ Sweatshirt - Of your university, favorite band, or fandom. With or without hood

☐ Turtleneck - In white, etc.

☐ Cable knit sweater - In white, etc.

☐ Sweaters - Turtle, mock turtle, round, or V-neck

☐ Sweater vest - To wear on its own or on top of shirts

☐ Shearling vest - To wear with skirts or jeans in fall

☐ Puffer vest - For fall

☐ Long black tank dress

☐ Floral dress

☐ Safari dress

☐ Black leather pants or leggings

☐ Black coated jeans

☐ Jeans - In white, light wash, medium wash, red, etc.

☐ Skinny cargo pants - In olive, etc.

☐ Trouser-cut jeans - For casual Fridays

☐ Wide-leg trousers - In black, camel, white, pinstripe, etc.

☐ Khaki pants

☐ Grid pants

☐ Leggings - In black, plaid, etc.

- ☐ Long black skirt
- ☐ Pleated midi skirt - In black, etc.
- ☐ Black circle skirt
- ☐ Floral A-line skirt
- ☐ Skirt suits

## SHOES & ACCESSORIES

- ☐ Foldable flats - To pack when you are wearing high heels
- ☐ Ballet flats - In nude, metallic, leopard, etc.
- ☐ Pointy flats - In nude, black, etc.
- ☐ Driving shoe
- ☐ Moccasins
- ☐ Toms
- ☐ Converse
- ☐ Vans
- ☐ Keds Champion original
- ☐ Superga
- ☐ Adidas Stan Smith
- ☐ Adidas Superstar

☐ New Balance retro sneakers - In black, gray, etc.

☐ Mary Janes

☐ Open-toe heels - In nude, black, snakeskin, etc.

☐ Pumps - In white, etc.

☐ Pointy heels - In nude, black, red, etc.

☐ Leopard heels

☐ Nude platforms

☐ Wedges - In nude, black, etc.

☐ Wedge sneakers - In nude, black, etc.

☐ Wedge boots - In black, etc.

☐ Peep-toe booties - In black, nude

☐ Flat boots - With hidden wedge if you are petite

☐ Ankle boots - In nude, white, brown, etc.

☐ Doc Martens

☐ Black combat boots

☐ Engineer or motorcycle boots

☐ Knee boots - In black, etc.

☐ Over the knee boots - In black, nude, etc.

☐ Hunter boots

☐ Tall boots - In black or brown

☐ Black baseball cap

☐ Black fedora

☐ Beret - In black, white, red, etc.

☐ Aviators

☐ Wayfarers

☐ Scarves

☐ Pashmina - In camel, etc.

☐ Skinny belt - In black, brown, metallic, red, leopard, snakeskin, zebra, etc.

☐ Chain belt - In gold and silver

☐ Black belt with grommets or studs

☐ Patent leather belt - In black, red, etc.

☐ Thick belt - In black, brown, etc.

☐ Leather or suede gloves

☐ Evening clutch

☐ Small cross-body bag - In black, beige, white, snakeskin, etc.

☐ Structured bag

☐ Hoop earrings

☐ Dangling earrings

☐ Statement earrings

☐ Delicate necklace with interchangeable pendants - In gold and silver

☐ Chunky chain-link necklace - In gold and silver

☐ Layered necklace - In gold and silver

☐ Statement necklace - Effortlessly dress up any plain outfit with this.

☐ Pearl necklace

☐ Diamond necklace

☐ Long necklace

☐ Collar necklace

☐ Choker

☐ Bangles

☐ Charm bracelet

☐ Cuffs - In gold, silver, black leather, etc.

☐ Bracelet - In gold, silver, etc.

☐ Tennis bracelet

☐ Ring - In gold, silver, etc.

☐ Cocktail ring

☐ Turquoise jewelry

☐ Brooch - To pin on your lapel, tee, bag, hat, etc.

# Epilogue

As I have illustrated in this book, a little goes a long way.

You do not have to buy the exact same item in the same brand, just something that looks like it. You probably have most of the items in this book in your closet. If not, you do not even have to buy brand new. Visit the local thrift shop and help the environment. Just make sure your clothes are in good condition, clean, and well pressed.

Clothes can do a lot for our image but also remember not to let other people's opinions determine your self-worth. I truly believe that we are all beautiful in our own way. So, always, always, always wear what makes YOU happy.

Hannah B.

# Credits

Book Producer: Xavier Basa; Photographer: Hannah B.

Black suit jacket from H&M. Denim jacket from Topshop. Black leather jacket (fur attachment removed) from H&M. Trench coat from Zara. Black wool coat from Pull & Bear. Black tank from Shein. White tee from Dynamite. Striped tee from Forever 21. White button-down shirt from H&M. Black turtleneck long sleeve from Shein. Little black dress from Dorothy Perkins. Black suit skirt from Daisy Fuentes. Black suit pants from Shein. Dark wash jeans (Joni) from Topshop. Black jeans (Joni) from Topshop. Black swimsuit by Ben de Lisi from Debenhams. Caftan from Ziya. Denim shorts (Mom Ultra High Denim Shorts) from H&M. Thong sandals from Planet. Black ballet flats from Aerosoles. White sneakers from Converse. Nude pumps from Kelly & Katie. Black pumps from H&M. Black ankle boots from Studio B. Black open-toe heels by H&M. Gold sequin dress by Shein. Gold open-toe heels by Urban Planet. White tank by Shein. Floral skirt by Urban Planet. Nude ankle boots by Ardene. Black romper by Old Navy. Cork wedges by H&M. Shorts suit by Shein. Teddy-lined suede cropped jacket by Shein. Leopard coat by Shein. Red pointy-toe heels by Forever 21.

# About the Author

Hannah B.'s mission is to help people decide what to wear in the morning and get the most use out of their clothes. She lives in Canada with her husband and daughter. Visit www.outfitsopedia.com for more details.

Hannah B.